RANKINS DRAGON

Everything You Need To Know About Rankins Dragons Feeding, Health Care, Habitat, Handling, Behavior And Much More.

BY

EDWIN ROBIN

COPYRIGHT © 2025 ALL RIGHT RESERVED

TABLE OF CONTENTS

CHAPTER 1: MEET THE RANKIN'S DRAGON

- Origins and natural habitat
- Differences between Rankin's Dragons and Bearded Dragons
- Why they make great pets

CHAPTER 2: UNDERSTANDING THEIR BEHAVIOR AND TEMPERAMENT

- Personality traits

- Social behavior
- Handling and taming tips

CHAPTER 3: CHOOSING YOUR RANKIN'S DRAGON

- Where to buy (breeders, pet stores, rescues)
- What to look for in a healthy dragon
- Male vs. female dragons

CHAPTER 4: HOUSING YOUR RANKIN'S DRAGON

- Enclosure size and setup
- Substrate choices
- Temperature, lighting, and humidity

CHAPTER 5: FEEDING AND NUTRITION

- Daily diet: insects, greens, and veggies
- Safe and unsafe foods
- Supplements and feeding schedule

CHAPTER 6:

HANDLING AND BONDING

- How to safely handle your dragon
- Building trust over time
- Fun activities and enrichment

CHAPTER 7: CLEANING AND MAINTENANCE

- Daily, weekly, and monthly cleaning tasks
- Preventing odors and bacteria
- Safe cleaning products

CHAPTER 8: HEALTH AND WELLNESS

- Common health issues
- Signs of illness
- When to visit a reptile vet

CHAPTER 9: SHEDDING, GROWTH, AND LIFESPAN

- What to expect during shedding
- Growth stages
- Life expectancy and signs of aging

CHAPTER 10: BREEDING RANKINS DRAGONS (OPTIONAL)

- Understanding breeding behavior
- Setting up a breeding environment
- Incubation and hatchling care

CHAPTER 11: TRAVELING WITH YOUR DRAGON

- How to transport safely
- Vacation care and boarding options
- What to pack

CHAPTER 12: FUN FACTS AND OWNER STORIES

- Unique quirks of Rankin's Dragons
- Real owner experiences
- Tips from seasoned keepers

CHAPTER 1:

MEET THE RANKIN'S DRAGON

If you're searching for a reptile companion that's charming, interactive, and slightly more compact than its more famous cousin, the Bearded Dragon, then the Rankin's Dragon might just be the perfect pet for you. Scientifically known as Pogona henrylawsoni, and often referred to as the Lawson's Dragon or Dwarf Bearded Dragon, the Rankin's Dragon is a lesser-known but equally delightful species that is gaining popularity in the reptile-keeping community.

These small, spunky reptiles hail from the arid and semi-arid regions of Queensland, Australia. Although their wild population is rare and not commonly observed in their native habitat, captive breeding has made them more accessible to enthusiasts around the world. What makes the Rankin's Dragon especially appealing is its manageable size, friendly nature, and low-maintenance care compared to larger reptiles.

Rankin's Dragons are often mistaken for juvenile Bearded Dragons due to their similar appearance. However, these dragons are a distinct species with their own set of characteristics. They typically grow to about 10 to 12 inches in length, making them significantly smaller than the more common Bearded Dragon (Pogona vitticeps), which can reach up to 24 inches. This more compact size makes them ideal for individuals who may have limited space or prefer a reptile that is easier to house and handle.

Despite their small stature, Rankin's Dragons have big personalities. They are curious, interactive, and generally quite tolerant of human interaction. Many owners report that their Rankin's Dragon will eagerly come to the front of the enclosure when approached, climb onto their hands, and even sit contentedly on their shoulder or chest. Their social nature and expressive behavior make them a joy to observe and care for, especially for beginner reptile keepers or families with responsible children.

What's particularly intriguing about Rankin's Dragons is their behavior. Unlike some reptiles that can be reclusive or skittish, Rankin's Dragons are known for being relatively bold and outgoing. They enjoy basking under their heat lamp, watching the world go by, and investigating anything new in their enclosure. These dragons are also diurnal, meaning they are active during the day, which aligns nicely with the routines of most people and allows for better interaction and bonding.

In terms of appearance, Rankin's Dragons have a rugged yet endearing look. Their bodies are covered in small, spiny scales, and they have a rounded head with a gentle, intelligent expression. While they do not have the long "beard" or throat pouch that Bearded Dragons are famous for, they may still puff out their throat slightly when feeling threatened or displaying dominance. Their coloration varies, but most exhibit earthy tones such as sandy browns, tans, and subtle oranges that help them blend into their natural environment.

Historically, Rankin's Dragons were not always readily available in the pet trade. Because of strict Australian export laws protecting native wildlife, these dragons are not legally exported from Australia. The ones found in captivity today are descendants of a small number of individuals that were brought out of the country before these regulations were put in place. As a result, the captive Rankin's Dragon population is relatively small, and maintaining genetic diversity has been a challenge. This makes responsible breeding practices incredibly important to the future of the species in the pet trade.

It's also worth noting that there has been some confusion over the years about the taxonomy of Rankin's Dragons. Some earlier literature classified them as a subspecies of the Bearded Dragon or even confused them with juvenile Bearded Dragons. However, they are now recognized as a separate species with their own behavioral traits, care requirements, and physical characteristics.

One of the most compelling reasons to consider a Rankin's Dragon as a pet is their adaptability to life in captivity. These dragons do not require enormous enclosures, and their dietary needs are simple and easy to fulfill. They thrive on a mix of live insects, leafy greens, and vegetables, and with the right lighting and temperature gradient, they can lead healthy, active lives. Their relatively small size means they're more economical to care for, requiring less food, a smaller enclosure, and fewer resources overall.

For individuals who are new to reptile ownership, Rankin's Dragons offer an ideal entry point. They are hardy creatures that can tolerate minor husbandry mistakes better than more sensitive reptiles. With that said, like all exotic pets, they do require specific conditions to thrive. Understanding their natural habitat and mimicking it as closely as possible in captivity is essential to ensuring their health and happiness. This includes providing appropriate heat, UVB lighting, hiding spots, and a clean, spacious environment.

Perhaps one of the most endearing aspects of owning a Rankin's Dragon is the bond that can form between pet and owner. While reptiles are not typically thought of as affectionate animals, many Rankin's Dragon keepers report a noticeable sense of recognition and trust from their dragons over time. These reptiles often become comfortable being handled, will climb onto their owner's hands voluntarily, and may even seem to enjoy sitting with their human companions for extended periods. This level of interaction sets them apart from many other small reptiles that prefer minimal contact.

Rankin's Dragons also exhibit a fascinating array of behaviors. From arm-waving (a submissive gesture) to head-bobbing (a dominant or mating signal), these actions can be both amusing and enlightening for the attentive keeper. Learning to read and interpret your dragon's behavior can enhance your relationship and ensure that their physical and emotional needs are met.

In conclusion, the Rankin's Dragon is a captivating and delightful pet reptile that offers many of the benefits of a Bearded Dragon in a smaller, more manageable package. They are friendly, interactive, and relatively easy to care for, making them an excellent choice for both new and experienced reptile keepers. While they may not be as widely available as some other reptiles, those who take the time to find a reputable breeder and invest in proper care will be rewarded with a pet that is both engaging and charming.

As we move through this book, we'll dive deeper into every aspect of Rankin's Dragon ownership—from setting up the perfect habitat and creating a balanced diet to handling tips, health care, and even breeding. Whether you're just starting out or looking to expand your knowledge, this guide will provide you with all the tools you need to become a confident and responsible Rankin's Dragon owner.

CHAPTER 2:

UNDERSTANDING THEIR BEHAVIOR AND TEMPERAMENT

One of the most captivating qualities of the Rankin's Dragon is its personality. While they may be small in size, these reptiles make up for it with charm, curiosity, and character. Understanding their behavior and temperament is essential for building a healthy and positive relationship with your pet and ensuring that they live a stress-free, enriching life in your care.

Rankin's Dragons are widely admired for their docile and friendly nature. Unlike many reptiles that can be shy or reclusive, Rankin's Dragons are often outgoing and quite social by reptilian standards. When well cared for and properly handled, they can develop a strong bond with their owners, recognizing them as a source of safety and food. Many owners report that their dragons greet them by approaching the glass of the enclosure or eagerly climbing onto their hands when offered the opportunity.

It's important to understand that, while Rankin's Dragons are generally gentle and calm, each dragon has its own personality. Some individuals are more inquisitive and active, while others may be laid-back and slow-moving. Much like people, they have their own moods and preferences, and getting to know your individual dragon will take some time and observation.

These reptiles are diurnal, meaning they are active during the day and sleep at night. During their waking hours, Rankin's Dragons spend much of their time basking under their heat source, exploring their enclosure, hunting live food, and occasionally interacting with their owners. Watching your dragon during these active hours will give you the best insight into their unique behaviors and preferences.

One particularly endearing behavior observed in Rankin's Dragons is what keepers refer to as "glass surfing." This is when the dragon stands on its hind legs and scratches or runs against the glass of its enclosure. While it may look like a playful or energetic act, it is usually a sign that something in the environment needs to be addressed. It could indicate stress, boredom, or even a desire to explore. While occasional glass surfing is nothing to worry about, consistent or frantic activity of this kind may suggest that the enclosure is too small, lacks stimulation, or that your dragon sees its reflection and mistakes it for another dragon.

Rankin's Dragons are also known for their expressive body language. One of the most recognizable behaviors is head bobbing, which is often used as a display of dominance or, during the breeding season, as part of courtship rituals. A male may rapidly bob his head to assert his presence or to communicate interest in a female. Conversely, females and submissive dragons may respond with a slower, gentler bob or an arm wave, which is an endearing, circular motion of one of the front legs that signals submission or peaceful intent. Watching these interactions is not only fascinating but also provides insight into your dragon's social instincts.

Another important behavior to be aware of is defensive posturing. Though rare in well-socialized dragons, a Rankin's Dragon that feels threatened or startled may puff up its body to appear larger, gape its mouth, or make short lunges to deter perceived threats. These actions are usually a last resort when the dragon is feeling cornered or unsafe. Avoid forcing interaction when these signs appear. Instead, give the dragon space and time to calm down. Patience, gentle handling, and consistent routines will go a long way in building trust.

Rankin's Dragons are not naturally aggressive toward humans. Biting is extremely uncommon and typically only occurs if the dragon feels extremely threatened or is mishandled. In most cases, biting is a result of fear, confusion, or mistaking a finger for food. Always wash your hands before and after handling your dragon and avoid hand-feeding insects without using tongs, especially when the dragon is excited or hungry.

Handling is a critical aspect of socializing your Rankin's Dragon. These reptiles tend to tolerate and even enjoy being handled, provided it's done correctly and regularly. Start slowly, allowing your dragon to get used to your presence. Let them approach your hand on their own terms rather than grabbing them suddenly. Support their entire body during handling, especially the tail and limbs, and never grab them by the tail or limbs as this can cause stress or injury. Over time, your dragon will learn that you are not a threat, and handling will become a pleasant experience for both of you.

Rankin's Dragons are also very intelligent. They can recognize feeding routines, differentiate between different people, and even learn from their environment. You might notice your dragon reacting to changes in lighting, movement outside their enclosure, or new decorations added to their habitat. They may also exhibit playful behaviors such as climbing branches, rearranging items, or observing activity around them. Enrichment is crucial for a Rankin's Dragon's mental health. Offering new textures, climbing options, hiding spots, and safe objects to explore will keep their minds and bodies engaged.

Interaction with other dragons is another area of their behavior worth discussing. While Rankin's Dragons are more tolerant of others than many reptiles, cohabitation should still be approached with caution. Males, in particular, can be territorial and may fight if kept together, especially in confined spaces. Females are generally more peaceful and may cohabit if provided with ample space, food, and separate basking areas. That said, even dragons that get along initially may develop dominance issues later on. Signs of bullying include one dragon consistently basking while the other hides, food hoarding, tail or limb nips, and general stress behaviors. For most keepers, it's best to house Rankin's Dragons individually unless breeding or under very carefully managed circumstances.

Sleep and resting habits are also important to observe. As mentioned, Rankin's Dragons are active during the day and will typically find a cozy, shaded spot to sleep at night. They may burrow slightly into their substrate, hide under decorations, or rest in elevated positions. A healthy dragon will have a consistent sleep-wake cycle that matches their lighting schedule. If you notice excessive lethargy during the day or unusual hiding, it may be a sign of stress, improper husbandry, or illness and should be investigated further.

Finally, let's talk about brumation. Brumation is a reptile's version of hibernation and is common in many lizard species, including Rankin's Dragons. This natural behavior typically occurs during the cooler months and involves a period of reduced activity, appetite, and sleepiness. Not all dragons go into brumation, and it can vary in intensity and duration. Some may just slow down a bit, while others may hide away for weeks or even months. If your dragon begins showing signs of brumation, it's important to monitor them closely, ensure hydration, and avoid force-feeding. Never attempt to wake a dragon in brumation unless advised by a veterinarian, especially if they are in good health and show no signs of distress.

Understanding the behavior and temperament of your Rankin's Dragon is essential to being a responsible and caring keeper. These little dragons have their own way of communicating and interacting with the world, and the more you observe and learn from them, the more rewarding your relationship will become. By paying attention to body language, providing appropriate enrichment, and practicing gentle, respectful handling, you'll create an environment where your dragon feels safe, confident, and curious. In the following chapters, we'll explore how to choose the right dragon, set up an ideal habitat, and provide the best nutrition possible—everything needed to ensure your Rankin's Dragon not only survives but thrives in your care.

CHAPTER 3:

CHOOSING THE RIGHT RANKIN'S DRAGON

Bringing a Rankin's Dragon into your home begins with an important decision—choosing the right individual. Although these small dragons are known for their friendly nature and manageable size, not all are created equal. Selecting a healthy, well-socialized Rankin's Dragon is the foundation of a successful and rewarding reptile-keeping experience. This chapter guides you through the entire process of choosing your dragon, from identifying a reputable source to recognizing signs of good health and avoiding common pitfalls.

Before you even step into a pet store or contact a breeder, it's crucial to do your homework. Understanding the needs of Rankin's Dragons, their ideal habitat, and care requirements is essential before committing to ownership. These reptiles can live for 6 to 10 years, sometimes longer with exceptional care, so your decision should be based on a long-term commitment. Once you're confident in your ability to provide for your future dragon, the next step is finding a reliable source.

Rankin's Dragons are not as widely available as their larger cousin, the Bearded Dragon, but they are increasingly offered by reputable breeders, exotic pet shops, and at reptile expos. Purchasing from a private breeder is often the best choice. Breeders who specialize in Rankin's Dragons tend to have more knowledge about the species and are more likely to produce healthy, well-socialized individuals. Ask around in online reptile communities, forums, or social media groups for recommendations. Attending reptile shows or expos can also give you the opportunity to meet breeders face-to-face, ask questions, and inspect the animals up close.

Pet stores can be hit or miss. Some maintain high standards of animal care, while others may house reptiles in poor conditions with inadequate lighting, improper diets, or overcrowding. If you choose to buy from a pet store, visit more than once and observe how they care for their animals over time. Pay attention to cleanliness, how knowledgeable the staff are, and the condition of the reptiles on display.

No matter where you're purchasing your Rankin's Dragon from, it's essential to examine the individual animals closely. Healthy dragons exhibit certain characteristics that are easy to identify once you know what to look for. First, observe their activity level. A healthy Rankin's Dragon is alert and curious, responding to movement and changes in its environment. It should not be lethargic or overly sluggish during daytime hours, especially under heat lamps when they are typically most active.

Inspect the body condition. A healthy dragon should have clear, bright eyes without any discharge. The skin should be smooth and free of lesions, retained shed, or scabs. Their limbs and tail should be fully intact—no visible kinks, deformities, or missing digits. The belly should be rounded but not bloated, and the tail should gradually taper and feel firm, not soft or wrinkled. A wrinkled or sunken tail can indicate dehydration or malnutrition.

The mouth and nostrils are also important to examine. The mouth should close fully and symmetrically, without bubbling, discoloration, or swelling. A gaping mouth while basking is normal, but continuous open-mouth behavior or wheezing could indicate respiratory issues. The nostrils should be clean and free from crusts or discharge.

Watch how the dragon moves. It should walk smoothly with coordination and strength. Limping, dragging limbs, or weakness may signal metabolic bone disease or injury. If the animal seems shaky, disoriented, or struggles to hold itself up, it may be suffering from calcium deficiency or neurological problems.

Age is another consideration. Hatchlings and juveniles are adorable and may seem like the most appealing choice, but they also require more careful husbandry. Their bones are still developing, and they are more sensitive to environmental conditions such as temperature, humidity, and diet. If you're a beginner, it may be wise to start with a juvenile or sub-adult Rankins Dragon that is a few months old and already well-established in feeding and growth.

Temperament is often easier to gauge in slightly older dragons as well. While hatchlings can be skittish, older dragons that have been handled regularly tend to be calmer and easier to socialize. Don't be afraid to ask the breeder or seller if you can observe the dragon being handled. A dragon that squirms a little at first is normal, but one that bites, hisses, or shows extreme fear may require more effort to tame.

Sexing your Rankin's Dragon may also be important, especially if you plan to house multiple dragons or avoid breeding. Males and females can generally be distinguished by their physical characteristics, though accurate sexing is usually possible only after a few months of age. Males tend to have broader heads, more prominent femoral pores (small dots along the underside of the thighs), and a thicker tail base due to the presence of hemipenes. Females generally have a narrower head and smaller pores. If you're unsure, a reputable breeder or exotic vet can help determine the sex.

Ask questions before committing to a purchase. A responsible breeder or seller should be able to tell you the dragon's age, diet, shed history, and any previous health issues. Inquire about the parents' health if possible, especially if you're buying from a breeder. Healthy lineage can reduce the risk of congenital issues and provide insight into the dragon's expected size and temperament.

Consider quarantine if you already own reptiles. A new Rankin's Dragon should be housed separately for at least 30 to 60 days while you monitor for signs of illness, parasites, or stress. This is a standard practice in responsible reptile keeping and protects your existing pets from potential infections.

Bringing your new dragon home is exciting, but preparation is key. Ensure that their enclosure is already set up and stable before their arrival. The habitat should include proper heat gradients, UVB lighting, hiding spots, climbing areas, and clean water. Avoid overwhelming your new pet with too much handling or interaction in the first few days. Let them acclimate to their new surroundings, explore at their own pace, and become comfortable with the sounds, lights, and rhythms of your home.

In the early days, monitor eating, basking, and stool patterns closely. A healthy, well-adjusted dragon will typically begin eating within a few days and show interest in basking and exploring.

Minor stress-related appetite suppression is normal at first, but anything beyond a week without eating should be addressed with a veterinarian experienced in reptiles.

Choosing the right Rankin's Dragon is not only about finding a healthy animal—it's also about finding one that fits your lifestyle and experience level. Patience, observation, and informed decision-making will help ensure that your new companion gets the best start in life. With the right choice and proper care, you'll gain a delightful pet with a charming personality and a strong bond that can last for years.

In the next chapter, we'll dive into setting up the perfect habitat for your Rankin's Dragon, exploring the essentials of heating, lighting, substrate, and enclosure design to ensure a safe and enriching home environment.

CHAPTER 4:

SETTING UP THE PERFECT HABITAT

Creating the perfect home for your Rankin's Dragon is one of the most vital aspects of their care. A well-constructed habitat not only provides for your dragon's basic needs but also fosters natural behaviors, keeps stress to a minimum, and supports long-term health and well-being. In this chapter, we will explore everything you need to know about setting up an ideal environment for your Rankin's Dragon—

from enclosure size and design to heating, lighting, substrate, and decor.

Rankin's Dragons, also known as Pogona henrylawsoni, are native to the arid and rocky environments of central Queensland, Australia. Their natural habitat is warm, dry, and full of crevices, rocks, and basking areas. Mimicking these environmental conditions in captivity is the key to keeping them healthy and happy. Fortunately, Rankin's Dragons are smaller than their Bearded Dragon cousins, which means they require less space, making them ideal for reptile keepers with limited room.

The first consideration in setting up your dragon's habitat is the enclosure itself. While Rankin's Dragons are relatively small—typically reaching 10 to 12 inches in length—a spacious enclosure is still important to allow for adequate movement, exploration, and thermoregulation. For a single adult Rankins Dragon, a glass terrarium with a front-opening design is ideal. A minimum size of 30 to 40 gallons is recommended, though larger enclosures, such as 36 inches long by 18 inches wide by 18 inches tall, are better for promoting activity. Front-opening terrariums make cleaning and interaction easier and help reduce stress during maintenance.

While smaller enclosures can be used for hatchlings and juveniles, keep in mind that they grow quickly, and upgrading the habitat as they mature will be necessary. Investing in the adult-sized enclosure from the beginning saves money and spares your dragon the stress of habitat changes.

Next, consider ventilation and security. Good airflow is important in maintaining proper humidity and temperature levels. Look for an enclosure with a screen top or well-designed vents. Ensure that the enclosure can be securely closed, as Rankin's Dragons are surprisingly curious and capable climbers. You don't want your pet escaping or other household pets gaining access to the enclosure.

Temperature regulation is another critical element of the habitat. As ectotherms, Rankin's Dragons rely on external heat sources to regulate their body temperature. A proper temperature gradient is essential, allowing them to move between warmer and cooler areas as needed. One end of the enclosure should serve as the basking area, with temperatures maintained between 100°F to 105°F. This can be achieved using a high-quality basking lamp positioned above a flat rock or basking platform.

The cool side of the enclosure should remain around 75°F to 85°F during the day. Nighttime temperatures can safely drop to around 65°F to 70°F. A ceramic heat emitter can be used during colder months or if your home gets too cool at night. Always use digital thermometers with probes or a temperature gun to accurately monitor the temperature at various points within the enclosure. Inaccurate temperatures are one of the leading causes of health problems in pet dragons, including poor digestion and metabolic bone disease.

Along with heat, UVB lighting is essential. Rankin's Dragons, like many reptiles, need access to ultraviolet B (UVB) light to synthesize vitamin D3, which is necessary for calcium absorption and bone health. Without adequate UVB exposure, they are at high risk for metabolic bone disease, a painful and often fatal condition.

Use a fluorescent UVB bulb specifically designed for reptiles, such as a T5 high-output bulb. The bulb should be mounted inside the enclosure, ideally 10 to 12 inches above the basking area, without any glass or plastic between the bulb and the dragon. UVB light should be provided for 10 to 12 hours a day, mimicking a natural daylight cycle. Replace UVB bulbs every six months, even if they appear to be functioning, as their UV output diminishes over time.

Humidity is another environmental factor to monitor. Rankin's Dragons do best in relatively low-humidity environments, consistent with their arid origins. Keep humidity levels between 30% and 40%. Use a hygrometer to track this, and avoid excessive misting or using substrates that retain too much moisture. Poor humidity control can lead to respiratory issues and skin problems.

Now let's talk about substrate—the material that lines the bottom of the enclosure. Substrate plays a role in hygiene, ease of cleaning, and natural behavior. For young dragons, the best option is reptile carpet, paper towels, or non-adhesive shelf liner. These options are easy to clean and eliminate the risk of accidental ingestion, which can lead to impaction—a serious blockage in the digestive tract.

For adults, some keepers prefer to use loose substrates such as a mix of play sand and organic soil, or specially designed bioactive substrate blends. While these can create a more naturalistic environment, they come with greater risk if not managed properly. If you choose a loose substrate, make sure your dragon is healthy, well-hydrated, and not prone to eating the substrate. Spot-clean regularly and change the substrate as needed to maintain hygiene.

Furnishing your dragon's enclosure is both practical and enriching. Provide a basking platform made of slate, tile, or a large rock beneath the heat lamp. Include multiple hiding spots, such as half logs, caves, or cork bark, especially on the cool side of the enclosure.

These give your dragon a sense of security and help prevent stress.

Branches, driftwood, and climbing structures are excellent additions as Rankin's Dragons enjoy climbing and surveying their environment from elevated spots. Make sure any climbing decor is stable and cannot collapse or shift under the dragon's weight. Artificial or live plants (non-toxic varieties) can also be used to enhance the habitat visually and provide additional hiding places.

Water is another key component of the habitat. Provide a shallow water dish that is easy to access but not deep enough for drowning. Change the water daily and scrub the dish regularly to prevent bacteria buildup. While Rankin's Dragons get most of their moisture from food, offering a water source is still important, especially in warm conditions.

You might also consider building a bioactive setup, especially if you're an experienced reptile keeper. Bioactive habitats mimic natural ecosystems and include live plants, a drainage layer, beneficial microfauna such as isopods and springtails, and specialized substrates. These systems can be more challenging to set up and maintain, but they reduce the need for deep cleaning and create a visually stunning, naturalistic environment.

Lastly, plan for cleaning and maintenance. Spot clean daily—remove feces, uneaten food, and shed skin. Deep-clean the entire enclosure monthly using a reptile-safe disinfectant. Remove all decor and substrate, wash everything thoroughly, and allow the habitat to dry completely before reassembling it.

Creating the perfect habitat for your Rankin's Dragon requires attention to detail, thoughtful planning, and a commitment to maintaining the proper environment day after day. However, once you've established a well-balanced enclosure with the right heat, light, humidity, and decor, your dragon will thrive—and you'll enjoy watching its natural behaviors, interactions, and unique personality emerge in a space that truly feels like home.

In the next chapter, we will explore the essentials of feeding and nutrition, ensuring your Rankin's Dragon gets a well-balanced diet to support its health from hatchling to adult.

CHAPTER 5:

FEEDING AND NUTRITION

Feeding your Rankin's Dragon is not just a daily task—it's an opportunity to support their health, build trust, and observe their unique behaviors and personality. Proper nutrition is the cornerstone of a healthy, long-lived Rankin's Dragon. From hatching to adulthood, what you feed your dragon—and how you feed it—affects its bone development, immune function, activity levels, and even its lifespan. This chapter will guide you through the essentials of feeding, including food types, appropriate feeding schedules, supplementation, hydration, and common feeding mistakes to avoid.

Rankin's Dragons are omnivores, meaning their diet consists of both animal-based and plant-based foods. In the wild, they consume a wide variety of insects, vegetation, and occasionally fruits or flowers. Replicating this diversity in captivity is crucial to ensuring they get all the necessary nutrients. However, their nutritional needs change as they age. Juveniles require more protein to support rapid growth, while adults thrive on a more plant-heavy diet that supports their metabolism and overall wellness.

Let's begin with insects, which are a primary source of protein. For young Rankin's Dragons (under six months old), insects make up the majority of their diet. Crickets and dubia roaches are the most common staples because they are high in protein, easy to source, and well-tolerated. Other suitable insects include black soldier fly larvae, silkworms, hornworms, and small mealworms (offered sparingly due to higher fat content and tough exoskeletons). Waxworms and superworms can be given as occasional treats but should never be a regular part of the diet because of their high fat content.

Always feed insects that are appropriately sized—no larger than the space between your dragon's eyes. Feeding insects that are too large can cause choking or impaction. Live prey should be active and healthy. Gut-loading insects 24–48 hours before feeding them to your dragon is essential; this means feeding the insects a nutritious diet so your dragon indirectly benefits from those nutrients. A mix of leafy greens, vegetables, and commercial gut-loading formulas can be used.

As your Rankin's Dragon matures, the emphasis on protein should gradually decrease. By the time your dragon is around 12 to 18 months old, the balance should shift to roughly 70–80% plant matter and 20–30% insects. This helps prevent obesity, fatty liver disease, and other complications associated with a protein-heavy diet in adult dragons.

When it comes to plant-based foods, not all greens and vegetables are created equal. Offer a wide variety of dark, leafy greens daily. Staples include collard greens, mustard greens, turnip greens, dandelion greens, and endive. These are rich in calcium and other nutrients essential for bone health and muscle function. Avoid iceberg lettuce and other watery greens that offer little nutritional value.

Vegetables such as squash, bell peppers, carrots (grated or finely chopped), and zucchini can be offered several times a week. Fruits should be treated as occasional treats due to their high sugar content. Small pieces of berries, mango, papaya, or apple can be given once or twice a week, but not more frequently. Overfeeding fruit can lead to digestive issues and weight gain.

All vegetables and greens should be washed thoroughly, chopped into manageable sizes, and offered fresh. You can lightly mist the greens with water to encourage hydration, especially in hot weather. Some dragons may prefer their greens slightly warmed or mixed with a few insects to spark interest, particularly if they are picky eaters or transitioning from a juvenile to adult diet.

A critical component of Rankin's Dragon nutrition is calcium and vitamin supplementation. In captivity, dragons cannot always produce enough vitamin D3 or absorb enough calcium from food alone, even with a good UVB lighting setup. A lack of these nutrients can result in metabolic bone disease (MBD), a debilitating and sometimes fatal condition that causes bone deformities, weakness, and seizures.

To prevent this, dust feeder insects with a calcium powder that includes vitamin D3 (if UVB exposure is not adequate) or without D3 (if your UVB lighting is strong and consistent).

Dust insects with calcium at least three to four times per week for juveniles and two to three times a week for adults. Additionally, a multivitamin supplement should be provided once a week for adults and twice a week for growing juveniles. Always use supplements made specifically for reptiles.

Another aspect of feeding is frequency. Juvenile Rankin's Dragons (up to six months old) are fed more often—typically two to three times per day. Insect feedings can be offered in the morning and again in the early afternoon, while greens should be available throughout the day. As the dragon grows, feeding frequency decreases. Sub-adults (six to twelve months old) can be fed once or twice a day. Adults (over 12 months) usually do well with one meal per day or every other day, depending on their weight and activity levels. Fresh greens, however, should always be available daily, regardless of age.

Be mindful of overfeeding, particularly with insects and fatty foods. An overweight dragon may appear sluggish, develop fat pads above its tail base, or have difficulty climbing. While a plump dragon might look cute, excess fat can lead to liver disease, reproductive issues, and joint strain.

Feeding can also be a great time to build trust and strengthen your bond with your dragon. Use feeding tongs to offer insects by hand or encourage them to eat from a dish. Watching your Rankin's Dragon hunt is not only fascinating—it stimulates natural behaviors and keeps them mentally and physically active. Just be cautious to remove any uneaten live insects after 15–20 minutes, as they can stress or even bite your dragon, especially during sleep.

Hydration is another important yet often overlooked part of nutrition. Although Rankin's Dragons get much of their moisture from food, they still need access to clean water. Provide a shallow water dish and change it daily. Many dragons do not drink standing water, so you may occasionally mist the enclosure lightly or offer water droplets on their snout with a syringe or dropper. You can also bathe your dragon in lukewarm water once a week to encourage drinking and help with hydration, digestion, and shedding.

Keep in mind that your Rankin's Dragon's eating habits can change with the seasons, age, and environment. Some dragons reduce their food intake during cooler months, especially if they enter a state of brumation (a reptilian version of hibernation). During this time, they may stop eating entirely for weeks. Monitor their weight and behavior, and ensure they remain hydrated even if they eat less. If appetite loss is sudden or unexplained, always consult a reptile veterinarian to rule out underlying health issues.

Finally, it's worth mentioning a few common feeding mistakes to avoid. Do not offer wild-caught insects, as they may carry parasites or pesticides. Avoid feeding your dragon dog or cat food, which contains unsuitable proteins and additives. Never feed fireflies, as they are toxic to reptiles. Be cautious with human foods or leftovers, as many contain salt, spices, and preservatives that are harmful to reptiles.

In conclusion, feeding your Rankin's Dragon is more than just offering a bowl of greens or tossing in a few crickets. It's about creating a balanced, varied, and age-appropriate diet that supports health, growth, and vitality. By understanding the nutritional needs of your dragon at every stage of life and feeding with care and consistency, you'll be laying the foundation for a happy, active, and long-lived companion.

In the next chapter, we'll dive into health care—how to recognize signs of illness, the importance of regular checkups, and tips for ensuring your Rankin's Dragon remains in peak condition for years to come.

CHAPTER 6:

HEALTH AND COMMON ILLNESSES

When it comes to keeping your Rankin's Dragon happy and thriving, nothing is more important than monitoring and maintaining its health. These hardy little reptiles are generally robust if kept in proper conditions, but like all animals, they are still susceptible to stress, disease, and nutritional deficiencies. As a responsible keeper, understanding the signs of good health, recognizing common health issues, and knowing when to seek veterinary care can mean the difference between a quick recovery and a life-threatening illness.

A healthy Rankin's Dragon is alert, active during daylight hours, and demonstrates a healthy appetite. Its eyes should be clear and bright, skin free of lesions or discoloration, and its body well-proportioned—not too thin or obese. Normal behavior includes basking under the heat lamp, climbing, exploring, and hunting live prey. You should also see regular, well-formed droppings, indicating a functioning digestive system.

It's important to conduct routine health checks on your dragon. Spend time observing it daily. Watch how it moves—is it walking confidently and without hesitation? Is it lifting its body off the ground with its legs fully extended?

Limping, lethargy, or dragging limbs could be signs of injury or disease. Open-mouth breathing, gaping, or wheezing could indicate respiratory problems, especially if accompanied by mucus or excessive saliva. A dragon that is consistently hiding, dark in coloration, or refusing to eat may be trying to communicate distress.

One of the most serious and unfortunately common issues among pet reptiles is Metabolic Bone Disease (MBD). This condition results from a calcium deficiency, often made worse by inadequate UVB lighting. Without enough calcium and vitamin D3, the body draws calcium from the bones, leading to softened, brittle bones that easily deform or fracture. Early signs include twitching limbs, tremors, soft jaw bones, and curved limbs or spine. If caught early, MBD can often be treated with dietary changes and supplementation, but severe cases may require veterinary intervention and long-term care. Prevention is the best approach—ensure your Rankin's Dragon has a diet rich in calcium and consistent access to high-quality UVB lighting.

Another potential issue is impaction, a condition where undigested material blocks the digestive tract. This can occur from eating oversized insects, ingesting loose substrate like sand, or consuming indigestible materials such as wood chips or gravel. Symptoms include lack of bowel movements, bloating, dragging of the hind legs, or complete lethargy. Mild cases may resolve with warm baths and gentle belly massages, but severe impactions require veterinary treatment. To prevent this, always feed appropriately sized insects, avoid loose substrate, and maintain correct basking temperatures to aid digestion.

Respiratory infections are also a concern, especially in enclosures with incorrect humidity or temperatures. Dragons kept in cold or overly damp environments are particularly vulnerable. Signs of a respiratory infection include labored breathing, wheezing, bubbling at the nostrils, and a general lack of energy. Treatment typically involves antibiotics prescribed by a reptile-savvy veterinarian, and it's crucial to improve environmental conditions to prevent recurrence.

Parasites—both internal and external—can also affect Rankin's Dragons. Internal parasites, such as pinworms or coccidia, may not show symptoms until the infestation is advanced. Look for signs like loose or foul-smelling stool, weight loss despite a healthy appetite, or bloating. External parasites, like mites, may be visible crawling around the eyes, mouth, or vent. They cause irritation and can transmit diseases. A fecal exam by a vet can confirm internal parasites, and treatment generally involves deworming medications. For external mites, enclosure disinfection and reptile-safe mite treatments are needed.

A common seasonal behavior that can be mistaken for illness is brumation—a natural state of dormancy, similar to hibernation, that occurs during cooler months. During brumation, Rankin's Dragons become less active, may refuse food, and spend more time hiding or sleeping. This can last from a few weeks to a few months. As long as the dragon is not losing weight rapidly and remains hydrated, brumation is normal and not harmful. However, it's important to distinguish it from actual illness. If you're unsure, consult a veterinarian.

Dehydration is another preventable condition that can quickly become dangerous. Signs include wrinkled skin, sunken eyes, lethargy, and a lack of urate (the white part of the poop). Always provide a shallow, clean water dish, and consider occasional misting or offering water droplets on the snout. Regular baths can help keep your dragon hydrated and also encourage them to drink.

Skin and shedding issues are relatively common. While most dragons shed easily and regularly, retained shed around the tail, toes, or eyes can cause circulation problems and even lead to loss of digits if not addressed. Soaking your dragon in lukewarm water and gently massaging stubborn areas with a soft toothbrush can help. Never pull or forcefully remove shedding skin. If a stuck shed becomes a recurring problem, review the humidity levels in the enclosure—Rankin's Dragons require moderate humidity, usually between 30%–40%.

On rare occasions, Rankin's Dragons may develop mouth rot (infectious stomatitis), which is characterized by swelling around the mouth, discolored oral tissue, excessive drooling, or visible pus. It is caused by bacterial infection, often due to minor injuries, poor hygiene, or a weakened immune system. Immediate veterinary care is required to prevent the infection from spreading.

Another issue to watch for is egg binding (dystocia) in females. Even females kept without a male can lay infertile eggs. If a female is straining to lay, appears bloated, restless, or is lethargic with no signs of egg-laying, she may be egg-bound. This is a medical emergency and requires prompt veterinary attention. Providing a proper lay box and ensuring good calcium levels can help reduce the risk.

Preventing illness is far easier than treating it, and good husbandry practices are your first line of defense. Maintain optimal temperatures with a proper basking gradient. Keep humidity levels within the recommended range. Clean the enclosure regularly, spot-cleaning daily and doing a deep clean at least once a month. Ensure UVB bulbs are replaced every 6 to 12 months depending on the brand, even if they still emit visible light—UVB radiation diminishes over time.

Always quarantine new reptiles for at least 30 days before introducing them into a shared space. This helps prevent the spread of unseen parasites or infections. During this period, monitor their behavior, eating habits, and stool quality closely.

Establishing a relationship with a reptile-experienced veterinarian is invaluable. Schedule an annual check-up, even if your dragon appears healthy. Early detection of issues can significantly improve outcomes. Take a fresh stool sample to each visit for parasite screening. Keep a record of your dragon's weight, feeding habits, and any behavioral changes to help your vet with diagnostics.

Finally, be attentive and trust your instincts. You know your dragon better than anyone. Subtle changes in behavior often precede physical symptoms. A Rankin's Dragon that seems "off" is worth a closer look. Acting quickly can save your dragon's life.

In summary, while Rankin's Dragons are generally hardy and resilient reptiles, they are not immune to health problems. Many common conditions—like metabolic bone disease, impaction, and respiratory infections—are preventable through proper husbandry, diet, and attention to environmental needs. By being proactive, observant, and responsive, you can catch health issues early and give your dragon the best possible chance at a long, comfortable life.

In the next chapter, we'll discuss handling and socialization—how to build trust, interact safely, and turn your Rankin's Dragon into a calm, confident companion.

CHAPTER 7:

HANDLING AND SOCIALIZATION

Rankin's Dragons are often described as one of the most personable and interactive pet lizards available, making them a fantastic choice for beginner and seasoned reptile enthusiasts alike. These reptiles are known for their curious demeanor, docile temperament, and willingness to interact with humans when properly socialized. However, building a strong, trusting bond with your Rankin's Dragon doesn't happen overnight—it takes patience, gentle handling, and an understanding of their behavior. In this chapter, we'll explore how to handle your dragon safely, how to socialize it properly, and how to interpret its body language to ensure positive interactions.

First and foremost, it's important to recognize that Rankin's Dragons, like all reptiles, are prey animals by nature. Even though they may seem relaxed and friendly, they are instinctively wary of potential threats. When a human hand reaches into their enclosure, especially from above, they may initially interpret this as a predatory action. This is why it's crucial to take a slow and respectful approach to handling, especially when your dragon is new to your home or unfamiliar with being touched.

When you first bring your Rankin's Dragon home, give it time to adjust to its new environment. This adjustment period typically lasts about a week, during which you should avoid handling and focus on providing a quiet, stress-free enclosure. Sit near the enclosure, talk softly, and allow your dragon to become accustomed to your presence. Observing you from a safe distance helps it build trust without feeling threatened.

Once your Rankin's Dragon is eating regularly and moving about its enclosure confidently, you can begin introducing gentle interaction. Start by placing your hand inside the enclosure without attempting to touch or pick it up. Allow your dragon to investigate at its own pace. This may take several sessions, but consistent exposure helps to build familiarity. Offer food from your hand or a pair of feeding tongs to create positive associations with your presence.

When your dragon appears comfortable around your hand, you can begin light handling. Approach from the side rather than from above, as this is less threatening. Gently slide your hand under its chest and support its body fully, including the tail if necessary. Avoid grabbing or restraining it tightly—gentle, confident movements are key. If your dragon attempts to run or resists handling, return it to the enclosure and try again another day. Never chase or force a dragon into handling; this only increases stress and slows the socialization process.

Short handling sessions are best at first—five to ten minutes is sufficient. Gradually increase the duration as your dragon becomes more relaxed. Handling sessions can take place once a day or every other day, depending on your dragon's comfort level. Over time, your dragon may become so accustomed to being handled that it willingly climbs into your hand or onto your shoulder.

During handling, be aware of body language cues that indicate stress or discomfort. A puffed-up beard, darkened body color, tail twitching, or a flattened posture can all be signs that your dragon is frightened or agitated. If you observe these behaviors, calmly return your dragon to its enclosure and allow it time to relax. With consistency, most Rankin's Dragons become very tame and even seem to enjoy exploring their surroundings outside of the enclosure.

Socialization goes beyond just being held. Allowing your dragon to safely explore a designated, secure area under supervision can stimulate its natural curiosity and increase its confidence. This can be a playpen-style area with enrichment items such as rocks, branches, or tunnels. Always ensure the area is free of hazards, including other pets, small objects they could ingest, or escape routes.

Some keepers even train their Rankin's Dragons to recognize feeding times or come when called using consistent verbal cues or tapping sounds. While they may not learn commands like a dog, they are intelligent enough to associate routine actions with rewards—like being picked up or fed. This can add an extra layer of bonding and engagement.

Children can also enjoy handling Rankin's Dragons, but supervision is essential. Teach children to be gentle, quiet, and patient, and never allow them to grab, squeeze, or chase the dragon. These lizards are small and delicate, and rough handling can cause injury or distress. It's also important to teach proper hygiene, such as washing hands before and after handling to prevent the spread of bacteria like Salmonella, which reptiles can sometimes carry.

If your Rankin's Dragon becomes unusually aggressive, this could be due to a variety of factors—brumation, hormonal changes, illness, or environmental stressors. Males, in particular, may become territorial or display dominance behaviors such as head bobbing or beard flaring during breeding season. Most of these behaviors are temporary and subside with time and proper care. If aggression persists, review husbandry conditions and consult a reptile-savvy veterinarian to rule out health issues.

It's worth noting that every Rankin's Dragon has a unique personality. Some may be naturally bold and outgoing, while others remain shy and reserved. Respecting your dragon's individual temperament is key to building trust. Not every dragon will enjoy being handled for long periods, and that's perfectly okay. The goal of socialization is not to force interaction, but to create a calm, trusting relationship where your dragon feels secure in your presence.

To support a positive handling experience, always handle your dragon in a warm environment. Reptiles are ectothermic and rely on external heat sources to regulate their body temperature. A cold dragon will be sluggish and may become stressed when handled. Handling should also be avoided right after feeding, as this can interfere with digestion or cause regurgitation. Similarly, avoid handling during shedding periods, as your dragon may be more sensitive or irritable.

Consistency is the cornerstone of socialization. Handle your dragon regularly and keep sessions calm and predictable. Use the same cues, approach, and handling techniques each time. This helps your dragon understand that it is safe and that you are not a threat. With time, your dragon may seek out interaction, explore you as part of its environment, and even nap on your lap.

In summary, handling and socializing a Rankin's Dragon is a deeply rewarding part of reptile ownership. It strengthens the bond between keeper and pet, provides mental stimulation for your dragon, and allows for health monitoring and interaction that enriches the lives of both parties. By respecting your dragon's boundaries, practicing gentle handling techniques, and providing positive experiences, you'll nurture a companion that is both tame and trusting.

In the next chapter, we'll explore the process of breeding Rankin's Dragons, including mating behaviors, egg-laying, and how to care for hatchlings.

CHAPTER 8:

BREEDING RANKIN'S DRAGONS

Breeding Rankin's Dragons can be an incredibly fascinating and fulfilling endeavor for dedicated reptile keepers. While not as commonly bred as their larger cousins, the Bearded Dragon, Rankin's Dragons (Pogona henrylawsoni) can breed successfully in captivity when given the right conditions and proper care. However, breeding is not to be taken lightly—it requires a solid understanding of their biology, behavior, and environmental needs, as well as a long-term commitment to the care of eggs, hatchlings, and potentially rehoming young dragons.

To begin, it is important to ensure that you have a compatible, healthy breeding pair. Males and females should be sexually mature before breeding, which typically occurs between 12 to 18 months of age. Earlier attempts to breed dragons that are too young or underweight can result in health issues, especially for females who must carry and lay eggs. A female should weigh at least 80 to 100 grams and be robust and active. Males are typically more muscular and have more pronounced femoral pores and hemipenal bulges at the base of the tail.

It is advisable to introduce the pair only during breeding attempts and not to house them together permanently. While Rankin's Dragons are more social than many other reptiles, cohabitation can still result in territorial aggression, especially in males. To determine sex before introducing the pair, examine the underside of the tail. Males will usually have two distinct bulges at the base of the tail (indicating the hemipenes), while females have a single bulge or a flatter area. Ventral femoral pores are also more prominent in males.

Before initiating breeding, some keepers simulate a short period of brumation—a natural dormancy period where the dragons slow down in activity and metabolism, mimicking a winter season. This is thought to trigger breeding instincts in the spring. To simulate brumation, reduce the photoperiod (daylight hours) and temperature slightly for 4 to 6 weeks. Dragons should remain hydrated and be monitored closely during this time. After the brumation period ends and temperatures and light are restored to normal, dragons are typically more receptive to mating.

When the male is introduced to the female, he may display courtship behaviors such as head bobbing, arm waving, tail twitching, and puffing up his beard. He may chase the female around the enclosure, biting the back of her neck to position her for copulation. These behaviors are normal, though they may seem aggressive to the uninitiated. The biting is usually part of the mating process, but close supervision is essential to ensure it doesn't escalate into harmful aggression. If the female seems overly stressed or is physically harmed, the male should be removed.

If mating is successful, the female will become gravid (egg-carrying) within a few weeks. She may show behavioral changes such as increased basking, restlessness, and digging behavior as she prepares to lay her eggs. During this time, it is crucial to provide a suitable nesting area. A lay box filled with a moist substrate such as coconut fiber, soil, or a sand/soil mix is ideal. The substrate should be deep enough for the female to dig—at least 4 to 6 inches.

Hydration and nutrition are critical during this stage. Provide calcium supplements daily to prevent deficiencies, and offer frequent meals rich in protein and leafy greens. A dehydrated or malnourished female may suffer from egg binding (dystocia), a serious and potentially fatal condition in which she is unable to lay her eggs.

When she is ready, the female will dig a tunnel in the lay box and deposit her eggs—anywhere from 8 to 20 per clutch, though some may lay more or fewer depending on age and health. Once she has finished laying, she will cover the eggs and exit the nesting site. At this point, it is important to remove the eggs carefully and transfer them to an incubator for proper development.

To incubate the eggs, place them in a sealed plastic container with a breathable lid, filled with a moist incubation medium such as vermiculite or perlite. The substrate should be damp but not wet—aim for a 1:1 ratio of water to substrate by weight. Bury the eggs halfway into the medium, ensuring they are stable but not submerged.

Eggs should be incubated at a consistent temperature between 82°F and 86°F (28°C to 30°C). Fluctuations can impact development, and temperatures above 90°F may cause deformities or death. Humidity should be maintained at around 75–85%. A small thermometer and hygrometer placed inside the incubator can help monitor conditions accurately. Candle the eggs (shine a light through them) around day 10 to confirm fertility—viable eggs will show a red or pink hue with visible blood vessels.

The incubation period lasts around 55 to 75 days, depending on temperature. Toward the end of incubation, the eggs may start to dimple slightly—a sign that hatching is near. Hatchlings will use an egg tooth to slit the shell and emerge over the course of several hours or even days.

Do not attempt to assist unless absolutely necessary, as premature intervention can cause harm.

Once hatched, baby Rankin's Dragons should be left in the incubator container until they absorb their yolk sacs and become more active. They can then be transferred to a nursery enclosure with proper heat, UVB lighting, and safety features. A small, shallow water dish and paper towel substrate work well for the first few weeks. Hatchlings are fragile and require close observation.

Feeding begins within a few days of hatching. Offer appropriately sized insects such as pinhead crickets, small roaches, or flightless fruit flies, dusted with calcium and vitamin supplements. Feed small amounts multiple times per day. As they grow, introduce finely chopped greens to promote balanced nutrition.

It's best to house hatchlings individually or in small groups to prevent bullying and competition over food. Rankin's Dragons are generally more tolerant of each other than some reptiles, but dominance hierarchies can still form, with larger individuals often intimidating or biting smaller ones. Keep enclosures clean and well-maintained to prevent illness, and monitor each hatchling's growth and behavior.

Raising baby dragons is both joyful and demanding. Some breeders choose to sell the young once they are a few weeks old and eating reliably. It is critical to have a plan for rehoming, as caring for multiple hatchlings long-term can be overwhelming. Ensure potential adopters are educated on care requirements and can provide suitable homes.

Breeding Rankin's Dragons also raises ethical responsibilities. Only healthy, genetically diverse individuals should be bred. Avoid breeding dragons that show signs of illness, deformities, or aggression. Reptile overpopulation is a real concern, and conscientious breeders must be mindful of contributing to the well-being of both their animals and the community of reptile keepers.

In summary, breeding Rankin's Dragons can be a rewarding venture that allows keepers to experience the full lifecycle of this captivating species. With attention to proper preparation, care, and responsibility, you can contribute to the healthy propagation of these gentle, inquisitive lizards while deepening your bond and knowledge as a reptile enthusiast.

CHAPTER 9:

COMMON HEALTH ISSUES AND HOW TO PREVENT THEM

As with all pet reptiles, Rankin's Dragons are susceptible to certain health issues that can impact their well-being. The key to maintaining a healthy dragon is prevention—providing a proper diet, appropriate habitat, and consistent care. Understanding the most common health issues and how to prevent or treat them will help ensure that your Rankin's Dragon remains happy and thriving for many years.

1. Metabolic Bone Disease (MBD)

Metabolic Bone Disease (MBD) is one of the most common health problems faced by pet reptiles, including Rankin's Dragons. This disease occurs due to a calcium deficiency, usually resulting from an improper diet or inadequate exposure to UVB lighting. Rankin's Dragons require a proper balance of calcium, vitamin D3, and phosphorus to maintain healthy bones. When these levels are disrupted, the bones become soft, fragile, and prone to fractures.

The most important preventive measure is providing sufficient calcium supplementation and UVB light. UVB rays help reptiles synthesize vitamin D3, which is crucial for calcium absorption. Without adequate UVB light, your dragon's body cannot process calcium effectively, even if you provide supplements. In captivity, it's recommended to use a high-quality UVB bulb that emits UVB rays at the proper wavelength (around 10-12%) and replace it every 6 months to ensure efficacy.

Calcium supplementation is also essential. You can provide this by dusting your Rankin's Dragon's food with calcium powder at least three times a week, with additional vitamin D3 supplementation. However, over-supplementation of vitamin D3 can cause toxicity, so use it sparingly. A balanced diet of greens and protein, such as crickets, dubia roaches, and leafy vegetables like collard greens, will help prevent imbalances in calcium and phosphorus.

Signs of MBD include soft or bent limbs, lethargy, difficulty moving, and twitching. If you notice any of these signs, consult a reptile veterinarian immediately. MBD is treatable if caught early, but if left untreated, it can cause permanent damage to your dragon's bones and joints.

2. Respiratory Infections

Respiratory infections are another common issue in Rankin's Dragons, typically caused by bacteria or fungi. These infections are often a result of improper temperatures or humidity in their enclosure. Rankin's Dragons are desert-dwelling reptiles and need a hot, dry environment to thrive. If they are exposed to damp, humid conditions for extended periods, it can lead to upper respiratory infections (URI), characterized by wheezing, nasal discharge, labored breathing, and lethargy.

The best way to prevent respiratory infections is by ensuring that your dragon's enclosure maintains proper temperature gradients and humidity levels. The basking area should be kept at around 100°F to 110°F (38°C to 43°C), with a cooler side of the enclosure ranging from 75°F to 85°F (24°C to 29°C). A humidity level of around 30-40% is ideal for Rankin's Dragons. Too much humidity encourages the growth of harmful bacteria and fungi, while too little can lead to dehydration.

If you suspect your dragon has a respiratory infection, it's essential to act quickly. Respiratory infections can quickly progress and become serious if left untreated. A reptile vet will likely recommend a course of antibiotics or antifungal medications to treat the infection. In addition to veterinary treatment, it's crucial to adjust the environmental conditions to prevent further health issues.

3. Parasites

Parasites are another concern for Rankin's Dragons, particularly if they are housed with other reptiles or if they come into contact with contaminated insects. External parasites such as mites, ticks, and internal parasites like roundworms and pinworms can affect your dragon's health. Parasites can cause a range of symptoms, including weight loss, lethargy, loss of appetite, and abnormal feces.

To prevent parasites, it's important to obtain feeder insects from a reputable source, ensuring that they are free of pesticides and contaminants. You should also quarantine new animals for several weeks before introducing them to your existing reptiles. Regularly cleaning and disinfecting the enclosure, along with providing a clean water source, will also help reduce the risk of parasite infestation.

If you suspect your Rankin's Dragon has parasites, it is essential to consult a reptile vet, who can run fecal tests and recommend the appropriate treatment. Common treatments may include deworming medications or topical treatments for external parasites.

4. Obesity

Obesity is a common issue in many pet reptiles, including Rankin's Dragons. Obesity often results from an improper diet—offering too many high-calcium or high-fat foods without enough activity. Rankin's Dragons, like all reptiles, require a balanced diet of protein, vegetables, and occasional fruit. When kept on a diet too rich in protein or fatty insects, or if they do not have access to a proper exercise area, they may gain excess weight. Overweight Rankin's Dragons may develop problems with movement, joint pain, and even metabolic disorders.

To avoid obesity, monitor the amount and type of food you offer your Rankin's Dragon. Dust insects with a calcium supplement, and provide a variety of leafy greens such as kale, collard greens, and dandelion greens. Make sure that the portion sizes are appropriate for their size and weight. It's also important to offer a large enough enclosure to allow for regular movement and exercise. A small, cramped living space can lead to a sedentary lifestyle, contributing to weight gain.

If you notice your dragon becoming overweight, try reducing the portion sizes of high-protein foods and increasing their exercise opportunities. If the problem persists, consult with a reptile vet for dietary guidance and further advice.

5. Shedding Issues

Like all reptiles, Rankin's Dragons undergo periodic shedding as they grow. During the shedding process, they may shed their skin in patches rather than all at once. Sometimes,

Rankin's Dragons may have trouble shedding properly, leading to retained shed, particularly around their feet, tail, or around the eyes.

Proper humidity levels are crucial for facilitating healthy shedding. If the humidity is too low, the skin may not come off easily, leading to retained shed. You can assist with the shedding process by providing a shedding box filled with moist paper towels or by lightly misting the enclosure. If you notice patches of retained shed, you can gently rub the area with a damp cloth to remove the skin.

If retained shed becomes a chronic problem or causes damage to the skin, it's important to consult a veterinarian. In some cases, excessive retained skin can lead to skin infections or circulation issues if left untreated.

6. Egg Binding (Dystocia)

Egg binding, or dystocia, is a serious condition that occurs when a female Rankin's Dragon is unable to lay her eggs. This condition is most often seen in females that are either underweight, dehydrated, or stressed. The eggs become lodged in the reproductive tract, leading to pain, swelling, and potential infection.

Preventing egg binding starts with proper nutrition and hydration. Ensure that your female Rankin's Dragon is healthy and properly fed before breeding. Providing a suitable nesting area is also important to ensure that the female has a place to lay her eggs when the time comes. If you suspect egg binding, take your dragon to the vet immediately. Treatment may include manual egg extraction, fluid therapy, or medication to encourage egg passage.

In conclusion, keeping Rankin's Dragons healthy requires a combination of proper diet, environmental care, and regular monitoring for any potential health issues. Early detection and intervention are crucial to preventing minor health problems from becoming more serious. By understanding the common health issues Rankin's Dragons face, you can provide a happy, healthy environment that will allow your dragon to thrive for years to come.

CHAPTER 10:

BREEDING RANKIN'S DRAGONS: A COMPLETE GUIDE

Breeding Rankin's Dragons can be an exciting and rewarding experience for responsible pet owners. These fascinating reptiles are relatively easy to breed in captivity when provided with the right conditions and proper care. However, breeding should not be taken lightly, as it requires substantial preparation, a deep understanding of their needs, and a commitment to ensuring the health and well-being of both the adults and the hatchlings. In this chapter, we will explore the essential aspects of breeding Rankin's Dragons, from understanding their reproductive cycles to caring for the eggs and hatchlings.

1. Understanding the Reproductive Cycle of Rankin's Dragons

Before considering breeding Rankin's Dragons, it is important to have a solid understanding of their reproductive cycle. Female Rankin's Dragons can begin to breed as early as 8 to 12 months of age, although it is recommended to wait until they are at least 18 months old to ensure that they are physically mature enough to carry and lay eggs. Males may be sexually mature at a similar age, but it is essential to ensure both reptiles are in optimal health before attempting breeding.

Breeding typically occurs during the warmer months of the year, as reptiles are highly influenced by environmental factors like temperature and light. In the wild, Rankin's Dragons are most active during spring and summer, when daylight hours are longer, and temperatures are higher. In captivity, it is essential to replicate these seasonal conditions by providing a temperature gradient, an appropriate light cycle, and the correct humidity levels.

A female Rankin's Dragon's reproductive cycle includes several key stages: mating, egg fertilization, egg laying, and egg incubation. The entire process can take several weeks to months, and it is crucial to monitor both the male and female closely during this time.

2. *Preparing for Breeding*

Preparation for breeding is crucial to ensuring a successful breeding cycle. Before breeding, make sure that both the male and female Rankin's Dragons are in optimal health. This means they should be well-fed, free of parasites, and living in a clean, stress-free environment. You should also ensure that the female is at a healthy weight and has access to a balanced diet of both protein and vegetables, as malnutrition can lead to egg-binding, a dangerous condition where the female is unable to lay her eggs.

Temperature and lighting are essential factors when preparing for breeding. You will need to provide a temperature range that mimics the natural environment of Rankin's Dragons. The basking area should be between 100°F to 110°F (38°C to 43°C), while the cooler side of the enclosure should be maintained between 75°F to 85°F (24°C to 29°C). A consistent 12- to 14-hour daylight cycle is also important to trigger their breeding behavior.

It is advisable to introduce the female to the male gradually and under supervision. Some Rankin's Dragons may be aggressive toward each other, especially the male, who may become territorial. However, with proper supervision, the female can choose when she is ready to mate. It is essential not to force the process, as stress can negatively affect both dragons.

3. Mating Behavior and Copulation

Once the female is introduced to the male, mating typically begins with courtship behaviors. The male will often engage in head bobbing, a territorial display that signals his interest. He may also attempt to bite the female's neck and chase her around the enclosure. This is a normal part of Rankin's Dragon mating behavior, but if the female shows signs of stress or aggression, it is important to separate them immediately and try again later.

When the female is receptive to mating, she will allow the male to mount her. Mating involves the male gripping the female's body with his hind legs and using his hemipenes (reproductive organs) to inseminate her. After successful copulation, the female will carry the sperm for several weeks, during which she will become gravid (pregnant) and begin to develop eggs internally.

It is important to provide a stress-free environment during this period, as excessive handling or environmental changes can disrupt the female's reproductive cycle. You should also monitor her weight and behavior, as a gravid female may exhibit different eating habits and increased rest periods.

4. Egg Laying and Nesting

After a period of 4 to 6 weeks, the female Rankin's Dragon will be ready to lay her eggs. It is essential to provide a suitable nesting area for her to lay the eggs in a safe and private space. This can be achieved by providing a laying box or a designated area filled with a substrate that allows for burrowing. A mixture of sand, coconut coir, and organic soil is ideal for egg laying, as it allows the female to dig and bury her eggs comfortably.

The female will instinctively seek out the nesting area when she is ready to lay her eggs. She will often dig a hole in the substrate, deposit her eggs, and then cover them up before leaving the nest. Rankin's Dragons typically lay a clutch of 6 to 15 eggs, but the number can vary depending on the individual.

It is crucial to remove the eggs from the nesting area carefully to avoid damage. Using a pair of soft tongs or a spoon, gently lift the eggs and place them in an incubation container. The container should be a shallow plastic box filled with a medium that retains moisture, such as vermiculite or perlite, which will help maintain the appropriate humidity levels during incubation.

5. *Incubation and Hatching*

Incubating Rankin's Dragon eggs requires careful attention to temperature and humidity. The ideal temperature range for incubating the eggs is between 80°F to 85°F (27°C to 29°C). A temperature higher than this may cause the eggs to hatch prematurely, while temperatures that are too low may cause the eggs to become unviable.

The humidity level should be maintained at around 70-80% to prevent the eggs from drying out. Too much humidity can lead to mold growth, while too little can cause the eggs to shrink and die. You can monitor the humidity by using a hygrometer and adjusting the humidity levels by lightly misting the incubator when necessary.

Incubation typically lasts between 60 to 90 days, depending on the temperature and conditions. During this time, it is essential not to disturb the eggs excessively, as this can interfere with the development of the embryos. Instead, check them regularly for any signs of mold or damage. If an egg appears to be infertile or is becoming moldy, it should be discarded to prevent contamination.

Once the incubation period is complete, the hatchlings will begin to break through their eggs. This process, known as piping, can take several hours. It is important to resist the temptation to help the hatchlings emerge from their eggs, as they need to do this on their own to strengthen their muscles and prepare for life outside the egg.

6. Caring for Hatchlings

After the hatchlings have emerged from their eggs, they will need to be provided with a separate enclosure from the adults. The enclosure should be warm, with a basking area of 100°F to 110°F (38°C to 43°C) and a cooler side of 75°F to 85°F (24°C to 29°C). They will also require a substrate that is easy to clean, such as paper towels or reptile carpet.

Hatchlings are small and delicate, so it is important to provide them with a diet of appropriately sized insects, such as baby crickets or small dubia roaches. Be sure to dust the insects with a calcium supplement to help promote healthy growth. Hatchlings should be fed multiple times a day, as they are growing rapidly during this stage of development.

It is also important to monitor the hatchlings closely for any signs of illness or injury, such as lack of appetite, lethargy, or difficulty moving. If any concerns arise, consult with a reptile veterinarian for guidance.

7. Conclusion

Breeding Rankin's Dragons can be a rewarding and educational experience, but it requires commitment, patience, and responsibility. It is crucial to ensure that both the adult dragons are in good health and that the breeding process is carefully monitored to avoid stress and injury. Providing the proper nesting and incubation conditions will give you the best chance of successfully hatching healthy baby dragons.

By following the steps outlined in this chapter and ensuring that you are well-prepared for the responsibility of breeding, you can enjoy watching your Rankin's Dragons grow into thriving, healthy adults. However, always be mindful of the long-term commitment involved in breeding reptiles, and make sure you are ready to provide for the hatchlings once they arrive.

CHAPTER 11:

HEALTH AND VETERINARY CARE FOR RANKIN'S DRAGONS

Like all reptiles, Rankin's Dragons are unique in their healthcare needs and require specific attention to maintain their overall health and well-being. Proper care, monitoring, and prompt attention to health issues can help ensure that your Rankin's Dragon lives a long, healthy life. Whether you are a new owner or an experienced reptile keeper, understanding the health risks and knowing when and how to seek veterinary assistance is essential. In this chapter, we will discuss the most common health issues that affect Rankin's Dragons, how to prevent them, and when to seek professional veterinary care.

1. Recognizing Signs of Illness

Rankin's Dragons are relatively hardy reptiles, but like all living creatures, they are susceptible to a range of health problems. One of the key aspects of keeping your Rankin's Dragon healthy is learning how to recognize the early signs of illness. Being able to spot symptoms early allows for quicker treatment and can often prevent more severe issues from developing.

Common signs that your Rankin's Dragon may be unwell include:

- *Loss of Appetite:* A sudden decrease in appetite can be a sign of illness, stress, or improper environmental conditions.

- *Lethargy:* If your dragon is less active than usual or seems excessively sleepy during the day, it could be a sign of an underlying issue.

- *Weight Loss:* Significant weight loss over a short period can indicate health problems such as parasites, poor nutrition, or digestive issues.

- *Abnormal Stool:* Diarrhea or constipation can be signs of gastrointestinal problems, parasites, or poor diet.

- *Respiratory Issues:* Labored breathing, wheezing, or nasal discharge are all symptoms of respiratory infections.

- *Skin Issues:* Dry, flaky, or discolored skin, or noticeable shedding problems can indicate improper humidity or potential infections.

- ***Swelling or Bloating:*** Swelling around the abdomen or limbs could indicate infections, injury, or internal parasites.

If you notice any of these signs, it is important to take your Rankin's Dragon to a veterinarian who specializes in reptiles. Timely intervention is crucial for successful treatment.

2. *Preventive Healthcare for Rankin's Dragons*

Preventing illness in Rankin's Dragons is far easier and more effective than treating it. Many health issues can be avoided through proper husbandry practices, including maintaining optimal environmental conditions, providing a balanced diet, and minimizing stress.

Environmental Conditions

One of the most critical factors in keeping your Rankin's Dragon healthy is ensuring that their enclosure mirrors their natural habitat as closely as possible. Proper lighting, temperature, and humidity are essential for the dragon's health.

- *Temperature:* Rankin's Dragons require a temperature gradient in their enclosure, allowing them to regulate their body temperature by moving between the warmer and cooler areas. The basking spot should be between 100°F and 110°F (38°C to 43°C), while the cooler side should range from 75°F to 85°F (24°C to 29°C). A proper temperature gradient supports healthy digestion, metabolism, and overall immune function.

- *Lighting:* UVB light is essential for Rankin's Dragons because it helps them synthesize vitamin D3, which is necessary for calcium absorption. Without UVB lighting, Rankin's Dragons can develop metabolic bone disease (MBD), a condition that can cause skeletal deformities and other serious health issues.

- *Humidity:* Rankin's Dragons need moderate humidity, typically between 30% and 40%. Humidity that is too high or too low can lead to shedding problems, dehydration, or respiratory infections.

Diet

A balanced diet is crucial for maintaining the health of your Rankin's Dragon. In the wild, they eat a variety of insects, small vertebrates, and plant matter. In captivity, their diet should consist of high-quality insects, such as crickets, dubia roaches, and mealworms, as well as a variety of leafy greens and vegetables. It's important to avoid feeding them insects that are too large, as they can cause choking or digestive problems. Supplementing their diet with calcium and multivitamins is also essential, especially if they are not exposed to adequate UVB light.

Regular Cleaning and Maintenance

Maintaining a clean environment is essential to preventing the spread of bacteria, parasites, and other harmful pathogens. The enclosure should be cleaned regularly, removing uneaten food, feces, and any other debris. Disinfect the enclosure every two to three weeks using reptile-safe cleaners. Additionally, ensure that all water bowls are cleaned daily to prevent bacterial growth.

Stress Management

Rankin's Dragons, like all reptiles, can become stressed by changes in their environment or handling. Stress can weaken their immune system and make them more susceptible to illness. Minimizing stress can be achieved by keeping the enclosure in a quiet area of the home, limiting loud noises and disturbances, and handling your dragon gently and only when necessary. Stress from improper housing or socialization can lead to behavioral and physical health problems, so maintaining a stable, comfortable environment is key.

3. Common Health Issues in Rankin's Dragons

Metabolic Bone Disease (MBD)
Metabolic Bone Disease is one of the most common health problems in reptiles, including

Rankin's Dragons. It occurs due to a deficiency of calcium or vitamin D3, often caused by inadequate UVB lighting or an improper diet. Symptoms of MBD include weakness, tremors, deformities of the bones (particularly the limbs), and softening of the jaw. MBD is a serious condition, but it can be prevented with proper UVB lighting and supplementation of calcium in the diet.

Respiratory Infections

Respiratory infections are common in reptiles and can be triggered by stress, improper humidity, or exposure to unsanitary conditions. Symptoms of respiratory infections in Rankin's Dragons include wheezing, labored breathing, nasal discharge, and lethargy. If left untreated, respiratory infections can lead to pneumonia and other severe complications. If you suspect a respiratory infection, take your Rankin's Dragon to a vet as soon as possible for diagnosis and treatment.

Parasites

Internal parasites, such as roundworms, tapeworms, and pinworms, can affect Rankin's Dragons if they consume contaminated insects or food. External parasites, such as mites, can also be a concern, especially if the dragon is housed with other reptiles or in an unsanitary environment. Symptoms of parasitic infestations include weight loss, bloating, diarrhea, or visible mites on the skin. A fecal exam by a veterinarian can determine if your dragon has parasites, and treatment typically involves medication to eradicate the parasites.

Shedding Issues

Rankin's Dragons shed their skin regularly as they grow. However, shedding problems can occur if the humidity levels are not maintained properly or if the dragon is stressed. Retained shed, particularly around the toes and tail, can lead to infections if not addressed. If your Rankin's Dragon has trouble shedding, increase the humidity in the enclosure and provide a shallow water dish or moist hide to encourage the shedding process. If the issue persists, gently remove the retained shed using a damp cloth, or consult with a vet if necessary.

Egg Binding (Dystocia)

Female Rankin's Dragons can experience egg binding, a condition where the eggs become stuck in the reproductive tract and cannot be laid. This can be caused by a variety of factors, including improper diet, stress, or lack of appropriate nesting sites. Signs of egg binding include lethargy, a swollen abdomen, and difficulty moving. If you suspect egg binding, it is important to seek veterinary care immediately, as this condition can be life-threatening if not addressed.

4. Seeking Veterinary Care

While Rankin's Dragons are generally hardy, there will be times when they require veterinary care. Finding a reptile-savvy vet is essential for proper diagnosis and treatment. Not all veterinarians have experience with reptiles, so it is crucial to choose one who specializes in exotic pets, particularly reptiles. You can ask for recommendations from local reptile clubs or online communities.

When seeking veterinary care, it is helpful to bring any relevant information, such as the dragon's diet, habitat conditions, and the symptoms you have observed. The vet will likely conduct a physical examination, take fecal samples for parasite testing, and may use imaging techniques to assess internal health issues. Early diagnosis and treatment are key to ensuring the best possible outcome for your Rankin's Dragon.

5. Conclusion

The health and well-being of your Rankin's Dragon should always be a priority. By providing a clean, stress-free environment, a balanced diet, and proper lighting and heating, you can prevent many of the common health issues that affect these reptiles. Recognizing the early signs of illness and seeking prompt veterinary care when necessary will ensure that your Rankin's Dragon enjoys a long, happy life.

Regular checkups with a reptile veterinarian, along with careful monitoring of your dragon's health, will help you stay ahead of potential issues and keep your pet in top form. With the right care, your Rankin's Dragon will thrive as an active, healthy companion for years to come.

CHAPTER 12:

BREEDING RANKIN'S DRAGONS

Breeding Rankin's Dragons can be a rewarding experience for knowledgeable and dedicated reptile owners. However, it requires careful planning, understanding of reproductive behavior, and attention to detail. Rankin's Dragons, like other reptiles, reproduce sexually, and their breeding process involves specific environmental conditions, a healthy pair, and an understanding of how to care for the eggs once they are laid.

In this chapter, we will explore the process of breeding Rankin's Dragons, including how to prepare for breeding, the breeding behavior of the animals, the incubation of eggs, and how to care for hatchlings. Additionally, we will touch on the ethical considerations involved in breeding and whether it is the right decision for you as a pet owner.

1. Preparing for Breeding

Before you even think about breeding your Rankin's Dragons, it is essential to ensure that both the male and female are healthy, well-cared for, and ready to reproduce. Breeding should not be taken lightly, as it requires time, effort, and commitment to both the adult dragons and the hatchlings that will follow. Here are some important factors to consider before breeding.

Health of the Parents

Both the male and female dragons must be in good health to breed successfully. Breeding unhealthy dragons can lead to complications such as infertile eggs, poor hatchlings, or even the death of one or both of the animals. Ensure that both dragons are free of parasites, infections, and other health conditions before attempting to breed them. A thorough check-up by a reptile-savvy veterinarian is recommended.

Age and Size

Rankin's Dragons typically become sexually mature around 8-12 months of age, though this can vary based on the individual dragon and environmental factors. It is important to wait until both dragons are fully mature before attempting to breed. Females that are too young or too small may struggle with egg production or laying, which can lead to complications such as egg binding. Males, on the other hand, may become overly aggressive if they are not mature enough for mating.

Environmental Conditions

To trigger the breeding season, Rankin's Dragons require specific environmental conditions. In the wild, these conditions would occur naturally with the change of seasons, but in captivity, you will need to replicate them. Breeding behavior in Rankin's Dragons is often prompted by the temperature and lighting changes.

During the breeding season, it is crucial to maintain a warm, well-lit environment with a temperature gradient in the enclosure. The basking spot should remain around 100°F to 110°F (38°C to 43°C), while the cooler side of the enclosure should be in the range of 75°F to 85°F (24°C to 29°C). In addition, providing UVB lighting is essential to help stimulate reproductive health and vitamin D3 synthesis.

Dietary Considerations

Before breeding, ensure that both dragons are receiving a well-balanced diet that supports their health and reproductive functions. Females should be provided with extra calcium and protein-rich foods in the months leading up to breeding to support egg production. This can include calcium supplements, such as calcium carbonate or calcium with D3, and protein-rich insects like crickets and dubia roaches. Additionally, providing a varied diet with plenty of leafy greens and vegetables will support both general health and fertility.

2. Breeding Behavior

Once the environmental conditions are right, and both dragons are healthy and ready, the breeding process can begin. It is essential to understand the mating behavior of Rankin's Dragons, as their courtship rituals and mating can sometimes be aggressive or intimidating to those unfamiliar with reptile behavior.

Courtship and Mating

Male Rankin's Dragons typically initiate courtship by displaying certain behaviors to attract a female. These behaviors may include head bobbing, arm waving, and displaying their colorful throat (dewlap). They may also engage in "mating dances" in which the male circles the female, trying to demonstrate his strength and dominance. If the female is receptive, she may display signs of acceptance, such as a calm posture and not attempting to flee. However, if she is not ready to mate or if she is not interested, she may show signs of aggression, such as puffing up her body or biting at the male.

Once a female is receptive, the actual mating occurs, where the male will mount the female. Mating typically involves the male gripping the female's sides with his claws while aligning his body to copulate. It can take several attempts for successful mating to occur. The male's reproductive organs are inserted into the female's cloaca, where sperm is transferred. After mating, the female will store the sperm for up to several months, allowing her to fertilize eggs over time as she prepares to lay them.

It is essential to monitor both the male and female during this period, as males may become overly persistent or aggressive towards the female. If aggression occurs, it may be necessary to separate the two dragons to prevent harm.

3. Egg-Laying and Incubation

After mating, female Rankin's Dragons will begin the process of producing eggs. This is an incredibly taxing process that requires the right environmental conditions to ensure successful egg-laying and incubation.

Gravid Females and Nesting Sites

Once the female has mated and fertilized eggs, she will enter a "gravid" (pregnant) stage, where her abdomen will begin to swell as the eggs develop. Gravid females may exhibit changes in behavior, such as becoming more reclusive or restless. During this time, providing a suitable nesting area is essential. Rankin's Dragons need a place to lay their eggs, usually a deep substrate or a special nesting box. Ensure that the female has access to a substrate that is deep enough for her to dig, such as a mix of moist soil, coconut fiber, or a similar material.

Without the right nesting area, female dragons may become stressed, which can lead to egg retention, egg binding, or even death. It is essential to provide a quiet, secure area where she feels comfortable digging and laying her eggs. Sometimes, they will dig several holes before they are ready to deposit their eggs, so patience and observation are key.

Egg-Laying

Once the female has selected her nesting site, she will begin laying her eggs. Female Rankin's Dragons typically lay 6-12 eggs in a clutch, though the number can vary. Once laid, the eggs should be gently removed from the enclosure and placed in an incubator to control temperature and humidity.

Incubation

The eggs should be incubated in a reptile egg incubator with a consistent temperature of around 85°F to 90°F (29°C to 32°C) and humidity levels of 80-90%. The eggs need to be kept moist, so it is important to maintain high humidity to prevent the eggs from drying out.

Depending on the temperature, it can take anywhere from 50 to 70 days for the eggs to hatch. It is important to regularly check the eggs for any signs of molding or other issues and to adjust the humidity levels as necessary.

4. Caring for Hatchlings

Once the eggs hatch, you will have baby Rankin's Dragons to care for. Hatchlings are incredibly small, measuring just a few inches long, and require special care to ensure their survival and growth.

Hatchling Enclosure

Hatchling Rankin's Dragons should be housed in a separate enclosure that has proper temperature and humidity levels. The basking spot for the hatchlings should be around 95°F (35°C), with the cooler side of the enclosure staying between 75°F to 80°F (24°C to 27°C). It is essential to provide plenty of hiding spots, as hatchlings can be easily stressed by the presence of other animals or too much activity. They also require access to UVB light, as they need to absorb calcium and develop healthy bones.

Diet

Hatchlings have small appetites and require small, soft foods that are easy for them to digest. You can offer them appropriately sized insects, such as pinhead crickets, small mealworms, and baby dubia roaches, as well as finely chopped leafy greens. Make sure to provide plenty of fresh water, as dehydration can be a concern for young reptiles. Calcium supplementation should be a part of their diet, especially as they begin to grow.

Growth and Development

Hatchlings grow quickly and will need frequent feedings to support their development. Monitor their growth, behavior, and health closely during this period, and provide a balanced diet to ensure proper growth.

5. Ethical Considerations in Breeding

Breeding Rankins Dragons comes with ethical considerations. It is essential to consider the responsibility of breeding and raising offspring before deciding to proceed. Breeding should only be done with the intention of improving the species' health and not for commercial purposes or financial gain. If you are not prepared to care for the hatchlings or find them suitable homes, it is better to refrain from breeding altogether.

Moreover, breeding can contribute to the overpopulation of reptiles, which is an issue in many areas. Many reptiles, including Rankin's Dragons, end up in shelters or are sold by breeders who do not have proper care, knowledge or resources. Therefore, it is critical to carefully consider your decision and make sure you have the knowledge, resources, and ethical intentions before breeding your Rankin's Dragons.

6. Conclusion

Breeding Rankins Dragons can be a fulfilling and educational experience, but it requires knowledge, preparation, and a commitment to the care and well-being of the animals involved. By understanding the process of mating, egg-laying, incubation, and hatchling care, and by considering the ethical implications of breeding, you can ensure a successful breeding experience that benefits both your dragons and the reptile community as a whole. Always keep the health and welfare of your dragons as your top priority throughout the breeding process.

Made in the USA
Monee, IL
20 May 2025